The

HEALING

Journal

Self-Discovery and Self-Care Practices
to Explore Your Inner World

PSYCHOLOGY BASED

LORENA LUCHIAN

Designed by Mădălina Dumitrescu

You can use the book for personal purposes. You should not sell, use, alter, distribute, quote, take excerpts, or paraphrase in part or whole the material contained in this book without obtaining the permission of the author first.

The author of this book does not prescribe medical advice or use any technique as a form of treatment for physical or medical problems without the advice of a physician, either directly or indirectly.

The author's intent is only to offer information of a general nature to help your exploration of wellbeing. If you use any of the information in this book for yourself, the author and the publisher assume no responsibility for your actions.

DEDICATION

*I dedicate this guide to **you***

for having the curiosity to go deeper into yourself.

This Journal Belongs to:

____

____

____

Contents

INTRODUCTION

Rumi (Poet)

Introduction

Do you wake up and feel excited about the day ahead?
Are you full of energy and enthusiasm?
Are you satisfied with your life?
Or maybe you try to connect to yourself on a deeper level?

Whatever your answer is, The Healing Journal will open your way to reflection and growth. This journal is a holistic guide for self-discovery, accompanied by self-care practices that will help you become the most inspired version of yourself.

By looking at the most important dimensions of your personality, you will (re)define who you are, see what works for you, and realize what you need to do to be happy and satisfied.

The tools and resources used in this journal are designed to change how you feel about yourself, your life, and your well-being.

The steps you will take in this journey...

Week One

You will put your story down on paper and see more clearly who you are.

Week Two

You will connect with your inner child and heal the non-love wounds.

Week Three

You will talk to your body and embrace its messages.

Week Four

You will become aware of your cognitive patterns and change your mindset.

Week Five

You will become aware of your emotional patterns and release what you no longer need.

Week Six

You will improve your lifestyle by taking decisions and actions to boost your health.

Week Seven

You will reconnect with your soul and access your loving energy.

Week Eight

You will explore your relationship(s) and do the work to find your balance.

Week Nine

You will examine your sensuality and connect with your feminine power.

Week Ten

You will become aware of your values and reflect on what is essential for you.

All these aspects of your personality are interconnected, influence each other, and make you who you are today.

Self-Discovery

Life is always giving you opportunities to look inside and see what gives you joy or what disrupts your inner peace. Life has its ups and downs; this is true. However, self-awareness is always the first step in the journey and can help you realize that challenges are paths which lead you to find your true self, if you are able to dive deeper. Only from that place can you remove old emotional layers and grow.

Self-Care

Everything becomes smoother and lighter when you feel connected to your inner self. Self-care does not just mean taking a bubble bath or spoiling yourself in a spa. Rather, it means to know who you are and then to cherish your body, emotions, thoughts, soul, and life.

Self-care is not selfish.

You will not become self-centered.

Instead, you will be happier. Your energy will increase and you will be more balanced. The self-care practices from this guided journal will make you bloom.

Reminder

I am here to remind you that you are the most significant person in your life. If you are happy, those around you will also be happy.

What happens in your life matches the energy you put out. The more you improve yourself and raise your vibration, the more you align with wonderful opportunities to nourish your body, mind, and spirit.

I have experienced and witnessed the importance of self-discovery in my practice. Many women who came to therapy with symptoms that looked like depression or anxiety realized that they had simply forgotten or didn't know how to take good care of themselves. And then something happened to wake them up: a divorce, a heartbreak, a diagnosis, extreme suffering, too much stress at work, deep dissatisfaction, or discontentment.

If you have difficult symptoms, don't ignore them. You might need treatment, but it can also happen that behind that sadness or anger, your soul – your true nature – is yearning for what is essential for you.

I often heard...

I didn't care about breathing until now, I didn't think of this before, or *Now I realize I also contributed to that...,* I didn't take care of my body and that's why I got sick, I was eating a lot because I was unhappy, I forgot that I like dancing so much.

The list goes on.

Take Responsibility for Your Life

You now hold this journal in your hands, which means you are ready to create space to grow in your daily life. Consider this space a sacred one, where you can allow yourself to feel, process, and release your feelings and correct your thinking.

The process is almost like therapy, where you have many insights and experience cathartic moments. You may come across uncomfortable feelings because the repressed emotions will finally find the space to come up as you open yourself. When this happens, open an imaginary window in the place in your body where you feel those emotions. Acknowledge them, then let them go away.

My Healing

I now understand that I chose to become a therapist to learn how to help myself first. It wasn't always easy to acknowledge my suffering, stay present when repressed emotions surfaced, or understand that a particular pattern which kept showing up was trying to alert me to something I had inside of me, hidden in the unconscious. It was only the work I did that brought me to a place of serenity, calm, and joy, regardless of what happened in my life.

Now I am happy to share what helped me find myself. I have created this insightful Healing Journal for you and I will guide you to explore your inner world.

What the Guided Journal Is Offering and How to Use it:

Ten weeks to examine your inner world. Each week you will focus on one dimension of your personality.

Weekly inspiring **quotes**.

Fifteen self-discovery questions for each of these dimensions to uncover your subconscious mind. Writing about your feelings and recalling your memories will put you in touch with your inner voice and help you to know your mind. All the questions are profound. Don't skip answering the ones you think aren't necessary. Fill in all the spaces – self-discovery also takes the courage to confront your repressed emotions.

From week two to week nine, you have **two beautiful self-care practices** mindfully chosen for you. Please insert them into your daily life. It's not enough to just read them. Do one exercise in the morning and the other in the evening, then write your insights into your daily self-care page.

Each **self-care page** (week two to nine) has spaces where you can write:

What you feel during the exercises.

The insights of the day.

The mood of the day.

Your affirmation.

And your ideas on how to take better care of that area of your life.

Are you ready? Changes happen when you step out of your comfort zone, which, as the name implies, isn't always comfortable.

Your goal is to have an authentic life: to feel free, happy, and in harmony with yourself. And this is what happens when you discover who you are, love yourself, and take care of yourself.

WEEK ONE

> *Identity cannot be found or fabricated but emerges from within when one has the courage to let go.*
>
> Doug Cooper (Writer)

Identity

Who are you? Where do you come from?

Identity is your self-image: the way you perceive yourself in this world. Your genes, family, environment, temperament, and experiences contribute to your personality and to the person you are today.

Write your bio starting with the characteristics you've gained from previous generations. These are the aspects you received from your family when you were born. Here you can include your name, place of birth, ethnic origin, religion, physical and biological characteristics, or predispositions. Write about your inherited medical and emotional vulnerabilities and psychological traits.

Then write about your acquired characteristics or achievements from the educational, social, professional, and personal point of view. Mention your interests.

This bio will help you see the whole picture more clearly. Be self-aware of your feelings.

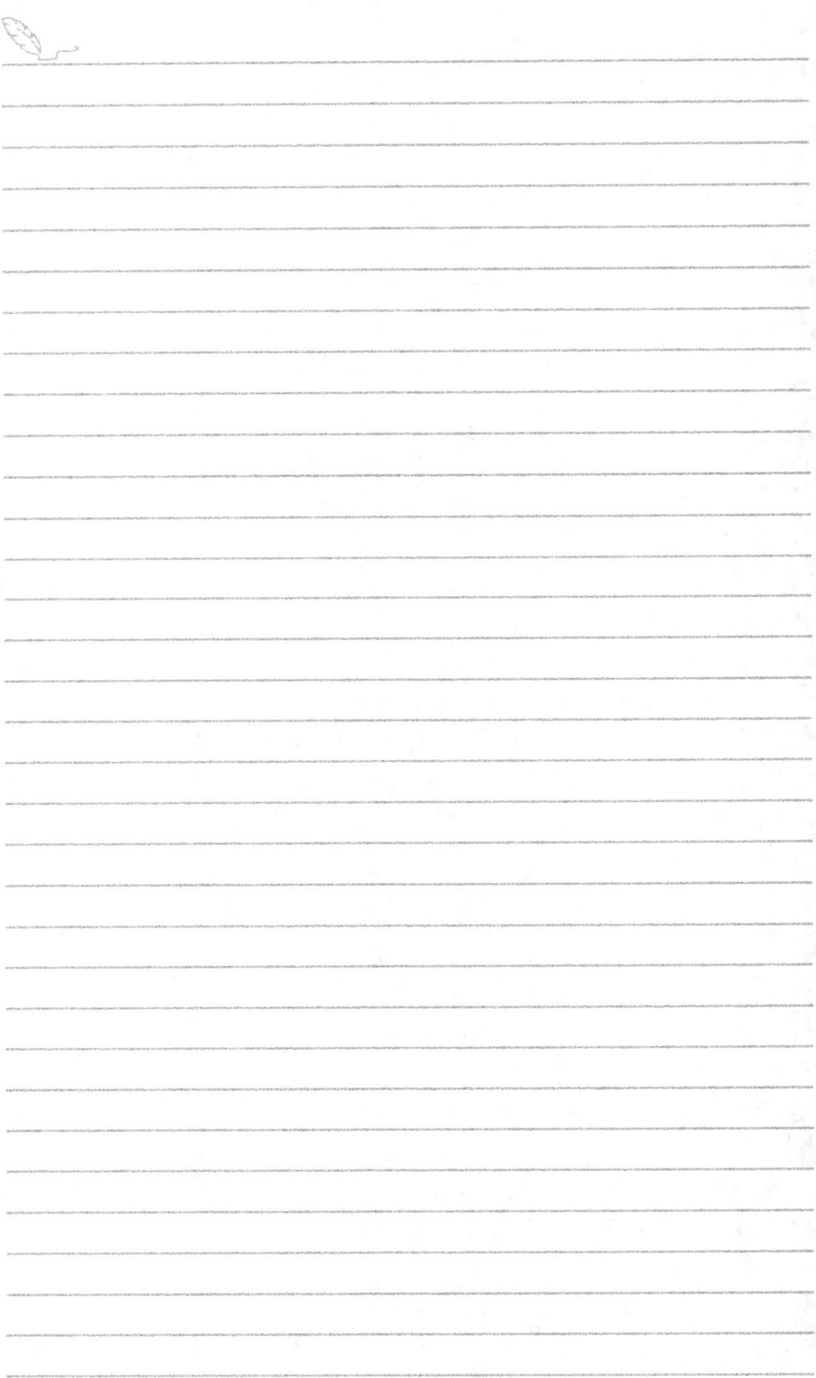

Now write your bio like a fairy tale. Use your creative side and place your story in the time and space you wish. Write about what happened to you in real life but transpose the facts into another dimension. You can play by describing the characters, the costumes, and the magic realms you like. You will unlock and release a hidden part of yourself. Observe your emotions.

WEEK TWO

> *Consciously, we are independent adults who are making our way in life. Unconsciously, the child in us decisively influences our perception, feelings, thinking, and actions much more than our reason does.*
>
> Stefanie Stahl (Psychotherapist)

Inner Child

Like everybody else, you have a little child inside of you. Your inner child holds all your memories and all the experiences you lived in your childhood. You don't consciously remember most of them but they are embedded in your subconscious mind.

The inner child is an essential part of yourself – fears, worries, and sufferings you had in the past influence your present. The pain you have experienced surfaces in your relationships as distress or difficulty meeting your own needs.

Working to heal and care about your inner child can help you alleviate many of the uncomfortable aspects you face today in your life and your relationships. To begin healing, you have to first acknowledge your inner child's presence and then patiently, gently, and lovingly grow and nourish this relationship.

Find a quiet place where you can relax. Connect with your inner child and let your answers flow:

1 Describe your relationship with your mother:

2 What did you learn from her?

3 Describe your relationship with your father:

4 What did you learn from him?

5 How would you describe the connection between your parents?

6 Were there any adults in the house as you grew up?
How were they?

7 Do you have siblings? If yes, describe your relationship
with them.

8 What was the most important relationship for you
as a child?

9 Who influenced you the most as a child and why?

10 What is your first memory as a child?

11 Did you feel loved by your parents (or significant adults)?

12 What did your parents do when you were upset or angry?

13 What is your favorite memory from your childhood?

14 What is the worst memory from your childhood?

15 Describe in a few words what kind of child you were:

Connect With Your Inner Child

 Close your eyes and relax your body. Let your eyes get heavier, unclench your jaw, and relax your cheeks. Lower your shoulders. Relax your arms and your hands. Soften your stomach.

 Feel your legs and feet get heavier and melt into more profound relaxation. Feel your body. Warm. Relaxed. Soft.

 Imagine yourself as a little girl.
Just observe her for a few seconds.
 Look at her hair, her body, and her eyes.
Notice her position, her attitude, and her expression.
 How old is she?
How is she dressed?
 What sounds do you hear her make?
What scent is around her?
 Where is she?
What is she doing?
 Is she happy?
Ask her what she needs.
 Listen to what she has to say.
Tell the child you love her unconditionally and give
her a gentle hug, full of kindness.
 Open your eyes and write your insights on your daily
self-care page.

Solving the Needs of Belonging and Security

Close your eyes and relax.

Go back mentally to a time in your childhood when you felt loved and protected.

Relive these beautiful, tender, comfortable, and delicate moments with those who took care of you.

Feel in your heart the safety, encouragement, and acceptance.

Feel the connection and know that you were loved and wanted in that moment.

If you don't have moments of closeness with your parents or relatives in your memory, you can choose imaginary parents.

Let your fantasy give you the parents you needed in your childhood; they can be real people, like a friend's parents, or imaginary characters.

Close your eyes and let your subconscious mind give you loving parents.

Imagine how happy the new parents are to have you and to be with you.

Let them behave as you needed in your childhood.

Give yourself a new, safe, and comfortable home.

Come back to this place whenever you need your parents.

Open your eyes and write your insights.

Daily Self-Care Page

Morning

Connect with your inner child

Evening

Solving the needs of belonging and security

Your ideas on how to take better care of your inner child

Insights

Affirmation

Daily Self-Care Page

Morning

Connect with your inner child

Your ideas on how to take better care of your inner child

Evening

Solving the needs of belonging and security

Insights

Affirmation

Daily Self-Care Page

Morning

Connect with your inner child

Your ideas on how to take better care of your inner child

Evening

Solving the needs of belonging and security

Insights

Affirmation

Daily Self-Care Page

Morning

Connect with your inner child

Your ideas on how to take better care of your inner child

Evening

Solving the needs of belonging and security

Insights

Affirmation

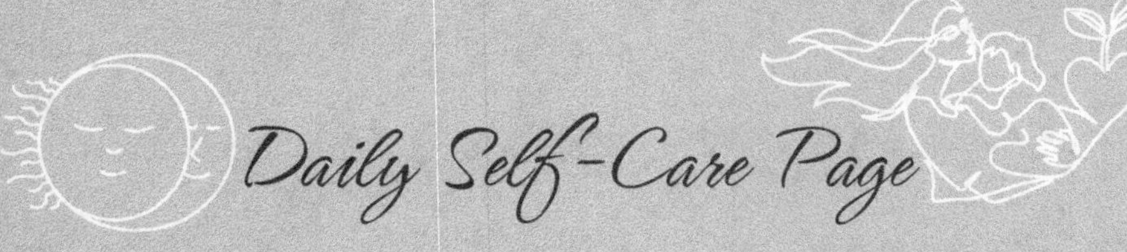

Daily Self-Care Page

Morning

Connect with your inner child

Your ideas on how to take better care of your inner child

Evening

Solving the needs of belonging and security

Insights

Affirmation

DAY: TODAY'S MOOD:

Daily Self-Care Page

Morning

Connect with your inner child

Your ideas on how to take better care of your inner child

Evening

Solving the needs of belonging and security

Insights

Affirmation

DAY: TODAY'S MOOD:

Daily Self-Care Page

Morning

Connect with your inner child

Your ideas on how to take
better care of your inner child

Evening

Solving the needs of
belonging and security

Insights

Affirmation

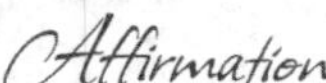

WEEK THREE

Nayyirah Waheed (Poet)

Body

You have an intimate relationship with your body but you don't always realize this. To know your body, you have to listen, receive, and embrace the messages you get.

The body takes the form of the emotions you have and of the thoughts you think. It cries at pain. It laughs when you are happy. It gets tense when you're stressed. It loosens when you relax. Deep in your body, you carry repressed emotions, needs, and anguish.

Are you in harmony with your body?

I love the quote of the poet Waheed. It gives me a sense of wholeness. It sounds like two parts of the same were fighting and, suddenly, they realized that the battle was over. Love and friendship replaced the negativity. What a beautiful attitude! You can learn to know and appreciate your body, to savor this special and unique relationship. Begin loving your body for what it *can* do. The body supports you and you must be grateful for its wisdom. Connect deeper to your body and listen to its whispers.

Find a cozy place, bring your attention to the body, and dive in:

1   What do you believe about your body?

2   How do you feel in your skin?

3   What did you feel regarding your body when you were a teenager?

4   Do you feel pain, tension, or discomfort in your body? If yes, where?

5   What is your body trying to tell you?

6   Do you consider your body your friend or your enemy?

____

____

____

____

7   What is your more significant fear regarding your body?

____

____

____

____

8   What part(s) of the body have you had problems with?

____

____

____

____

9   Do you feel pleasant sensations in your body?
If yes, where?

____

____

____

____

10   What part of your body do you cherish the most?

____

____

____

____

11   What makes you attractive?

12   How does your body like moving?

13   What can you do to make your body happier?

14   How are you moving?

15   How would your life be different if you learned to love
and respect your body?

Love Your Body

Fall in love with your body. It is yours and it's the only one you have.

Mentally send vibrant energy to the whole body.

The body is connected to your feelings and your thoughts. Bring your attention to your heart.

Open your heart and love your body as it is now – from the top of your head to the tips of your toes.

Let your consciousness heal and harmonize your body.

Love all the cells of your body.
Love all your organs.
Love your muscles and bones.
Love your skin.

Spend at least five minutes loving your body without thinking of anything else.

Notice how you feel now.

Breathing and Releasing Physical Tensions

Close your eyes and relax.
Tighten your right fist and arm, contracting the muscles of your arm but keeping the rest of the body relaxed.

Do not tighten your jaw at the same time.

Observe how the tension is accumulating and notice the sensations as they occur.

Now release and relax all the tension from your arm and hand, while loosening your entire body a little bit more.
With closed eyes, receive the sensations that arrive.

Give a name to these perceptions (heat, tingling, sensation of heaviness, lightness).

Now do the same for the whole body.

Begin by breathing out fully, emptying the stomach and lungs.

Breathe in deeply and slowly to the tips of your toes.
Hold your breath, bring your hands above your head, and tense the whole body, the face, the throat, the shoulders, the abdomen, the buttocks, and the legs. Become aware of all the muscles.

Tense a little bit more and, at the same time, notice the sensations arising from the accumulated tension.

Hold for a few seconds and then exhale all the air from the chest and belly. Relax your body, bring your hands down, and release all tension with each out-breath.

Repeat ten times and notice how you feel after the exercise.

Daily Self-Care Page

Morning

Love your body

Evening

Breathing and releasing physical tensions

Your ideas on how to take better care of your body

Insights

Affirmation

Daily Self-Care Page

Morning

Love your body

Your ideas on how to take better care of your body

Evening

Breathing and releasing physical tensions

Insights

Affirmation

DAY: TODAY'S MOOD:

Daily Self-Care Page

Morning

Love your body

Your ideas on how to take better care of your body

Evening

Breathing and releasing physical tensions

Insights

Affirmation

Daily Self-Care Page

Morning

Love your body

Your ideas on how to take better care of your body

Evening

Breathing and releasing physical tensions

Insights

Affirmation

Daily Self-Care Page

Morning

Love your body

Evening

Breathing and releasing physical tensions

Your ideas on how to take better care of your body

Insights

Affirmation

Daily Self-Care Page

Morning

Love your body

Your ideas on how to take better care of your body

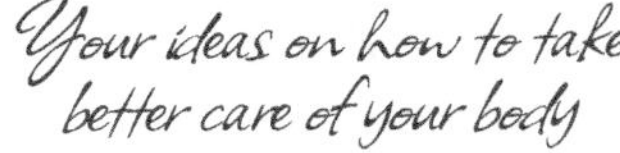

Evening

Breathing and releasing physical tensions

Insights

Affirmation

DAY: [____]   TODAY'S MOOD: [____________]

Daily Self-Care Page

Morning

Love your body

Your ideas on how to take better care of your body

Evening

Breathing and releasing physical tensions

Insights

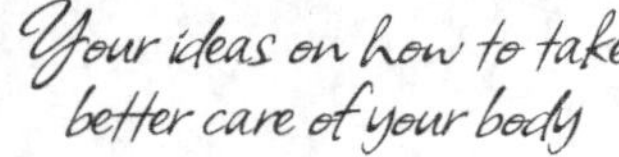

Affirmation

WEEK FOUR

> *All the things that truly matter, beauty, love, creativity, joy and inner peace arise from beyond the mind.*
>
> Eckhart Tolle (Spiritual teacher)

Mind

We continue with the discovery of the mind.

Due to its ceaseless activity, the mind pulls you away from what you are and disconnects you from your being. Every thought and feeling you have creates a vibration in your body. Thoughts can be so powerful that they can even affect your biology and make you feel happy or frustrated.

Self-awareness is the answer to a calm, balanced, and stable mind. What is the benefit of letting your mind wander and picking up the negative? It is only going to make you lose your center.

You have to observe your mental atmosphere and focus your attention on pleasant thoughts that make you feel good.

Self-observation brings about profound changes in neuronal activity. Most of your thoughts are impulsive when you are not conscious of yourself. The subconscious lies behind your conscious mind and contains all the programs, ideas, and beliefs you didn't even know you had. Let them come out along this self-discovery process and you will have a clearer image of what your mind produces. Then, you can focus on what you want and what you need to make your life more beautiful.

Go to your quiet place and discover your subconscious mind:

1   What do you believe about yourself?

____

____

____

2   What are some of your self-limiting beliefs?

____

____

____

3   Is your mind hyperactive? What kind of thoughts dominate your thinking?

____

____

____

4   How would you characterize your thinking patterns?

____

____

____

5   What are the usual stories created by your mind?

____

____

____

6 How does your thinking make you feel?

7 What do you think you need to be happy?

8 What worries you?

9 How could you solve that problem?

10 Is your thinking rigid or flexible?

11 Can you disconnect from your mind?

12 I want

13 I should

14 I like

15 I don't like

Self-Care Practices

Sophrology Exercise

Sit comfortably, close your eyes, and let yourself drown in the flow of thoughts. Follow them.

They "run" from one notion to another, multiplying endless ideas and creating a story.
Notice what you feel and where...
And now, bring your attention inwards.
Become aware of your body, your breath, and your physical sensations.
Move your attention from your mind to your body.
Fill the body with your entire attention.
Become aware of your breath and your physical sensations, savoring the perceptions given by the depth of your being.
Be here, now, for a few minutes, leaving all thoughts to one side.
Even if they appear, keep your attention on the body, from the top of the head to the tips of the toes...

Observe how you feel now and stay a little bit more connected to your body.

Complaining feels good only for a short time but has become a habit for many people. Negative thoughts overwhelm your mind and create "storms" in your head.

Count your blessings instead of thinking of what you don't like. The more you concentrate on the negative, the more you'll see only that. Focusing on the positive side will raise your energy and make you feel more optimistic and confident.

What you give your attention to really matters. Counting your blessings is an excellent mental cleaning practice. Gratitude can significantly impact your life – if you do it all the time. It can make you happier and more generous with yourself and others.

Thinking, emotions, and body fuse together. Only you can decide in which direction you want to turn your attention.

Daily Self-Care Page

Morning

Sophrology exercise

Evening

Be grateful

Your ideas on how to take better care of your mind

Insights

Affirmation

Daily Self-Care Page

Morning

Sophrology exercise

Your ideas on how to take better care of your mind

Evening

Be grateful

Insights

Affirmation

Daily Self-Care Page

Morning

Sophrology exercise

Your ideas on how to take better care of your mind

Evening

Be grateful

Insights

Affirmation

Daily Self-Care Page

Morning

Sophrology exercise

Evening

Be grateful

Your ideas on how to take better care of your mind

Insights

Affirmation

Daily Self-Care Page

Morning

Sophrology exercise

Your ideas on how to take better care of your mind

Evening

Be grateful

Insights

Affirmation

Daily Self-Care Page

Morning

Sophrology exercise

Your ideas on how to take better care of your mind

Evening

Be grateful

Insights

Affirmation

Daily Self-Care Page

Morning

Sophrology exercise

Evening

Be grateful

Your ideas on how to take better care of your mind

Insights

Affirmation

WEEK FIVE

> *Feeling sad about anything*
> *is holding onto it.*
> *—This is something I have to let go of*
> *and immediately you will feel better.*

Lester Levenson

(Physicist and modern master)

Emotions

Emotions are subjective and transitory states associated with thoughts, feelings, behavioral responses, and a degree of pleasure or displeasure. Emotions do not depend only on situations but also on what you think about those situations – such as interpreting their potential for threat or happiness.

Bodily reactions accompany emotions. For example, when you are surprised, you open your eyes and mouth and raise your hands to the face. Your body is connected with your mind and thinking. You can only feel your emotions in the body.

What do you do with all the emotions, especially with negative and repetitive ones? You try to ignore, deny, and suppress your feelings most of the time. Still, eventually they come out one way or another – and when they surface, you think you lose control.

Go to your favorite quiet place. Become aware, contemplate, and embrace your emotions as they appear:

1   Do you notice any emotions connected to your body?

2   For example, do you have a contraction in your chest related to something you're resisting?

3   Or maybe a sense of warmth and excitement in your heart?

4   What is your emotional atmosphere?

5   What disturbs you the most?

6   How does this make you feel?

7   Are you often hurt?

8   Where do you feel the hurt in your body?

9   Do you let yourself feel and process your emotions?

10   How do you react when you feel overwhelmed by your feelings?

11 Where there are uncertainties and pressures, you always:

____

____

____

____

12 Which model from your family have you taken on when expressing or not expressing emotions?

____

____

____

____

13 When do you feel angry, disappointed, or frustrated?

____

____

____

____

14 When do you feel happy, satisfied, or joyful?

____

____

____

____

15 What would you like to improve regarding your emotional life?

____

____

____

____

Self-Care Practices

Be Kind and Do a Good Deed Every Day

If you want to be happy, be kind.

Acts of kindness make you happier and healthier. They relieve the symptoms of depression and even help you live a longer, healthier life.

Happiness hormones are released in the brain when you are kind, helping lift your mood and make you feel more positive and optimistic.

Kindness is good for those who receive it, but it's good for the giver, too.

Pay kindness forward. If someone does something for you, do something kind for someone else. A simple act can bring a smile to a person's face for a whole day.

Kindness to yourself is the most important form of kindness. It is simply caring for your needs, having self-compassion and self-love.

Release Technique

Think of a situation that's agitating.

Notice what you feel.

Disconnect from your head and thoughts by moving your attention in the body.

Feel the unwanted emotion and imagine it is an energy that needs to be released.

Open an imaginary door or window in the stomach or chest area to feel the emotion and let the energy leave.

Or you can imagine the disagreeable energy going out like smoke from a fireplace, like a cloud moving up, or like a volcano erupting.

It may be difficult to acknowledge your deep-rooted feelings, but they will leave if you give them permission.
As you let go, you will feel lighter and lighter.

Daily Self-Care Page

Morning

Be kind and do a good
deed every day

Evening

Release technique

Your ideas on how to take
better care of your emotions

Insights

Affirmation

Daily Self-Care Page

Morning

Be kind and do a good deed every day

Evening

Release technique

Your ideas on how to take better care of your emotions

Insights

Affirmation

Daily Self-Care Page

Morning

Be kind and do a good deed every day

Evening

Release technique

Your ideas on how to take better care of your emotions

Insights

Affirmation

Daily Self-Care Page

Morning

Be kind and do a good deed every day

Evening

Release technique

Your ideas on how to take better care of your emotions

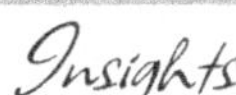

Insights

Affirmation

Daily Self-Care Page

Morning

Be kind and do a good
deed every day

Evening

Release technique

Your ideas on how to take
better care of your emotions

Insights

Affirmation

Daily Self-Care Page

Morning

Be kind and do a good deed every day

Evening

Release technique

Your ideas on how to take better care of your emotions

Insights

Affirmation

Daily Self-Care Page

Morning

Be kind and do a good
deed every day

Evening

Release technique

Your ideas on how to take
better care of your emotions

Insights

Affirmation

WEEK SIX

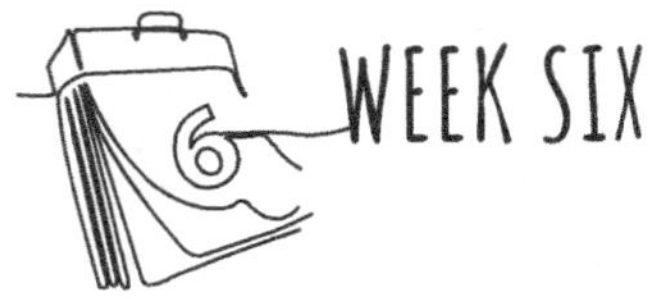

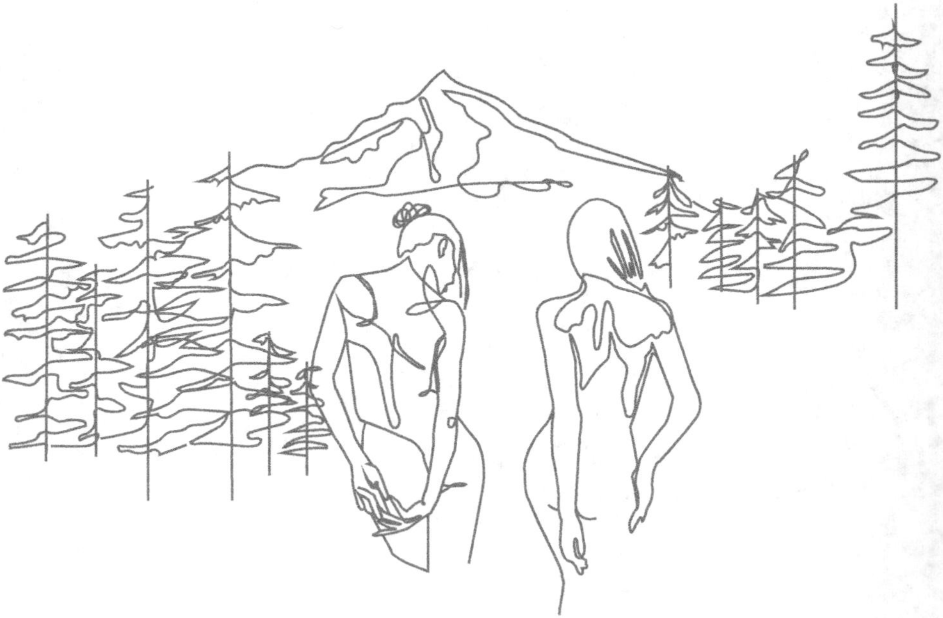

*If you want to change attitudes,
start with a change in behavior...*

William Glasser (Psychologist)

Behavior

Self-care behavior, a key concept in health promotion, refers to decisions and actions to improve your health at all levels.

Examples of self-care behaviors include reading books, attending classes, exercising, seeing a doctor regularly, getting more rest, lifestyle changes, following healthy diets, seeking alternatives, and making decisions to act. It is vital to take good care of your body, mind, and soul every day, not just when you get sick. Learning how to eat right, reduce stress, exercise regularly, and take a time-out when you need it is essential to self-care and can help you stay healthy and happy.

To maintain a healthy, flexible body and mind, you need to joyously move to get your heart pumping and keep your body fluids and qi circulating.

Research shows that people who recharge and restore are more creative, pleased, and successful. Please answer the following questions sincerely. You will have a clearer idea of what you need to change or do differently regarding your lifestyle.

1 What motivates you to action?

2 When do you act? In what circumstances?

3 How would you describe your behavior (in general)?

4 How many times a week do you exercise or move your body?

5 Do you engage in stress-reducing activities (excluding TV or time spent on screens)?

6   What activities give you joy and pleasure?

7   Do you engage every week in such activities?

8   Do you spend time in nature?

9   Do you make time to relax? (Not just when you sleep.)

10   How many hours per night do you sleep?
Do you wake up refreshed?

11 Do you eat a whole foods-based diet rich in colorful fruits and vegetables?

12 Do you drink enough water?

13 Do you feel nourished, healthy, and strong?

14 Do you get enough social time with people who make you happy?

15 On a scale of one to ten, where are you regarding your health and well-being (10 is maximum)?

Self-Care Practices

Conscious Walks

Walks are pleasant and easy ways to diminish stress and move your body.

Walks can grow your awareness while you slow down enough to concentrate your attention on your body and breathing.

Noticing the familiar environment, as if you're seeing it for the first time, allows you to keep your mind open and create time and space.

While walking, expand your attention to sounds.
Then shift your attention to your sense of smell.
After a few minutes, move your attention to vision, colors, objects, and whatever else you see.

Also note the senses of touch and taste.

With each step and each breath, you become more present and aware of all your senses. Let your body remember the less complicated periods of your life.

Prepare a Delicious Healthy Meal and Take Pleasure in Food

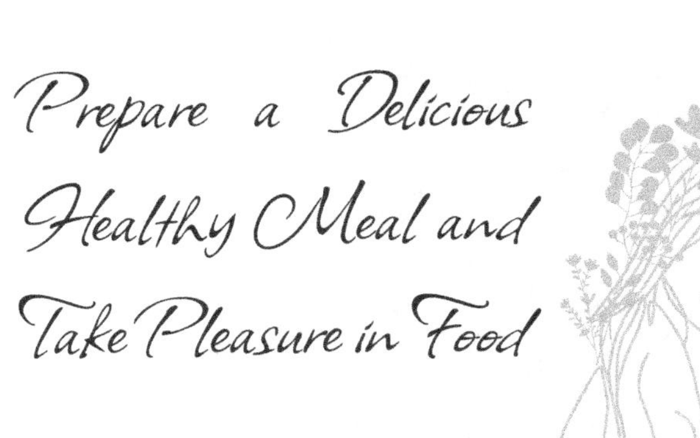

Healthy eating can definitely change your life.

Food is part of your daily life – you have to nourish yourself every day, not just once in a while.

Eating your favorite but bad-for-you foods and participating in activities that provide instant gratification isn't a self-care behavior.

But adopting healthy lifestyle habits that can be maintained long-term and eating a healthy diet is.

Every time you practice cooking, you are practicing one of the most fundamental forms of self-care.

Daily Self-Care Page

Morning

Conscious walk

Your ideas on how to take better care of your lifestyle

Evening

Prepare a delicious healthy meal and take pleasure in food

Insights

Affirmation

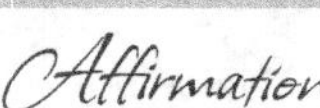

Daily Self-Care Page

Morning

Conscious walk

Evening

Prepare a delicious healthy meal and take pleasure in food

Your ideas on how to take better care of your lifestyle

Insights

Affirmation

Daily Self-Care Page

Morning

Conscious walk

Your ideas on how to take better care of your lifestyle

Evening

Prepare a delicious healthy meal and take pleasure in food

Insights

Affirmation

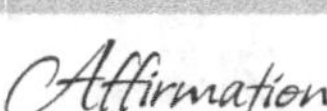

Daily Self-Care Page

Morning

Conscious walk

Your ideas on how to take better care of your lifestyle

Evening

Prepare a delicious healthy meal and take pleasure in food

Insights

Affirmation

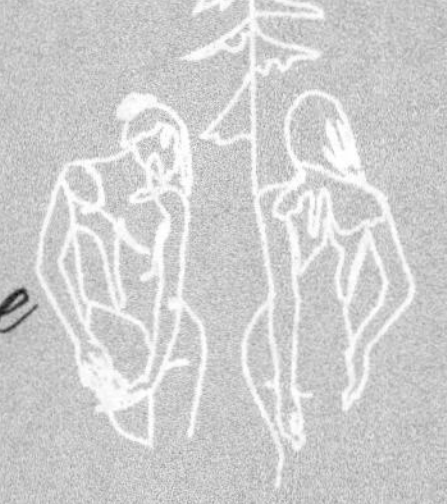

DAY: TODAY'S MOOD:

Daily Self-Care Page

Morning

Conscious walk

Evening

Prepare a delicious healthy meal and take pleasure in food

Your ideas on how to take better care of your lifestyle

Insights

Affirmation

DAY: TODAY'S MOOD:

Daily Self-Care Page

Morning	Evening

Conscious walk

Prepare a delicious healthy meal and take pleasure in food

Your ideas on how to take better care of your lifestyle

Insights

Affirmation

Daily Self-Care Page

Morning

Conscious walk

Your ideas on how to take better care of your lifestyle

Evening

Prepare a delicious healthy meal and take pleasure in food

Insights

Affirmation

WEEK SEVEN

> *At any moment, you have a choice, that either leads you closer to your spirit or further away from it.*

Thich Nhat Hanh

(Zen master)

Spirituality

Spirituality is taking care of your soul. It is a loving attitude toward what your inner self needs to be nourished and fulfilled. If you don't listen to your soul, you deeply bury the messages of your authentic self.

Spirituality gives you meaning and purpose in life. It includes a sense of connection to something bigger than yourself. It is your relationship with the Divine.

Spirituality can also be described as the feeling and the attitude of love and compassion for yourself, other people, animals, and the planet.

Spirituality is faith and protection. It can be considered a journey that leads you from fear to love. The more helpful, loving, and caring you are with yourself and with other beings on the planet, the more spiritual you are.

Please sit in your sacred space and contemplate the questions, finding the answers in your soul and heart rather than in your mind.

1   What is your relationship with the Divine?

2   Do you trust life?

3   Do you follow your intuition?

4   What does your soul want to tell you?

5   Are you well and at peace most of the time?

6   What is your purpose in life?

7   Is faith part of your life?

8   How loving are you?

9   Which is the biggest lesson your ego learned?

10   How can you contribute to a better world?

11 Do you treat yourself with kindness and compassion?

12 Do you treat others with kindness and compassion?

13 What is your one wish for the world?

14 What is sacred for you?

15 What is spirituality in your own words?

Self-Care Practices

Practice Love

Practicing love is the most powerful way to change how you feel and to change your life at large.

Love is inside you: you can find it if you let go of the non-love feelings. Love feels wonderful, non-love hurts.

Just for now, access the love you have inside and immerse your whole being in it.

Love yourself first.

Love with all your heart. When you are loving, you are happy.

Love more instead of waiting to be loved.

Then extend love to each member of your family, to your friends, colleagues, and all the people.

Love the earth, the animals, the plants, and the solar system. Love yourself and watch what happens in your life. Love is the answer.

Faith

"Change me, Divine Beloved, into one who always trusts where You guide me.

May I always have faith in following Your lead.

Let me bless my life's unfolding in all the ways that are right for me.

May I always know that all is occurring in Divine Order and every need is always met in the right time and way.

May I always trust You.

May I always know We are one."

DAY: TODAY'S MOOD:

Daily Self-Care Page

Morning

Practice love

Your ideas on how to take better care of your soul

Evening

Prayer

Insights

Affirmation

Daily Self-Care Page

Morning

Practice love

Evening

Prayer

Your ideas on how to take better care of your soul

Insights

Affirmation

Daily Self-Care Page

Morning

Practice love

Evening

Prayer

Your ideas on how to take better care of your soul

Insights

Affirmation

Daily Self-Care Page

Morning

Practice love

Evening

Prayer

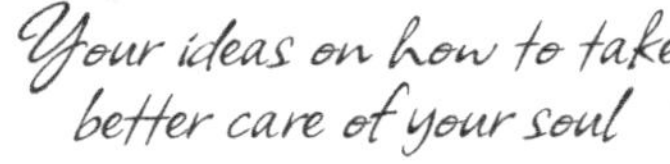
Your ideas on how to take better care of your soul

Insights

Affirmation

Daily Self-Care Page

Morning

Practice love

Evening

Prayer

Your ideas on how to take better care of your soul

Insights

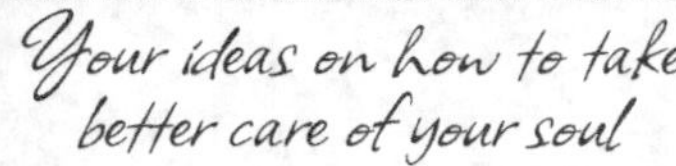

Affirmation

Daily Self-Care Page

Morning

Practice love

Evening

Prayer

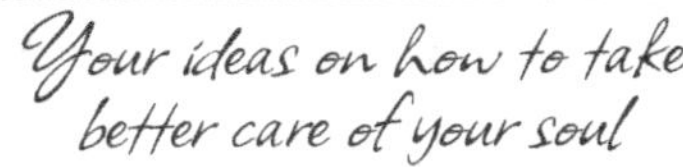

Insights

Affirmation

# Daily Self-Care Page

DAY: TODAY'S MOOD:

Morning

Practice love

Evening

Prayer

Your ideas on how to take better care of your soul

Insights

Affirmation

WEEK EIGHT

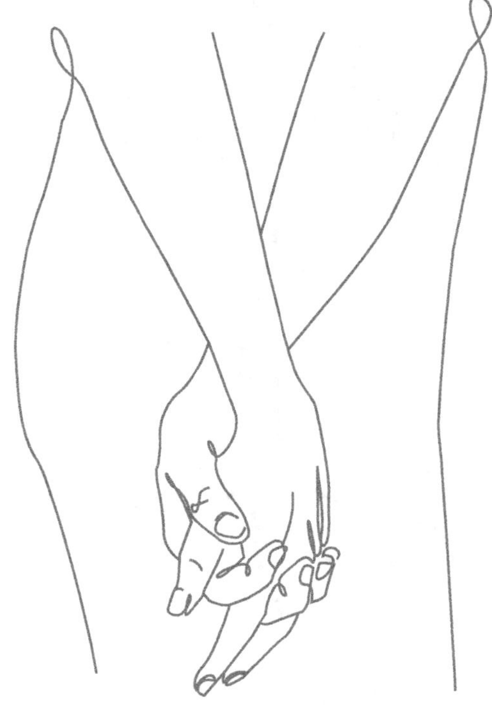

There's no perfect relationship.
All relationships are work.
If you put in the work, you'll
reap the rewards.

Jesse Metcalfe

(Actor)

Relationships

Everybody dreams of having excellent, vibrant, loving relationships. So why do so many people live alone or in relationships that lack closeness and interest in each other?

Is that the case for you? Do you expect unhappy people to make you happy?

The truth is that they can offer you only what they have. If you wait for others to change, you'll have to wait forever.

The good news is that there's another way. Work with yourself to become a better partner. Raise your vibration and let go of the non-love feelings. When you know who you are and you love yourself, you can also be more present and loving towards your partner. In this way, you change your vision and your energy shifts from neediness to wholeness. When you are not afraid anymore, the new, positive climate you create will also strengthen the bond of your relationship.

Take time to reflect on your relationship (or relationship pattern) and answer these questions sincerely:

1   What is the pattern of your relationship(s)?

2   What is your biggest wish regarding your relationship(s)?

3   What frightens you?

4   You feel deprived of...

5   What do you need more of right now?

6   What do you need less of?

____

____

____

7   What is causing you to feel resentful and why?

____

____

____

8   When do you feel yourself in your relationship(s)?

____

____

____

9   What do you argue about most of the time?

____

____

____

10   Where do you make mistakes?

____

____

____

11 Thinking that your partner is your mirror, what is it in you that you don't want to see?

12 What can you do to improve your relationship(s)? What is up to you?

13 Do you have unconscious expectations that your partner will fulfill childhood deficiencies?

14 Describe your partner in a few words.

15 How would your partner describe you?

Approval

Think of a person you have a problem with...
Right now, you are creating a lot of negativity in your mind and body. How can you have a relationship with someone you don't get along with?

If you do not do what I want, I criticize you, judge you, blame you; this is your attitude about acceptance and love.

Now, try not to disapprove of that person. Do it for yourself, not for them.

Give them as much approval as possible. You don't have to agree with what they say or do.

Approve of that person as much as you can in your heart because you do not want the energy of disapproval to be present in you.

Now that you are aligned with the approval energy, continue sending approval to the person. And more. And even more. Do it for at least five minutes. (Set your cell to ring after five minutes.)

Then you'll notice that the person you were thinking of is smiling at you. And, most importantly, you will feel much better.

Forgiveness

Forgiveness is a process that takes place inside of you.

Forgiveness is an act of kindness toward yourself and is good for your mental and emotional health.

If you want to feel lighter, you need to release that heavy feeling that dwells in your body – called resentment.

Write a letter to someone who you think needs to be forgiven, then burn it. Seven days, seven letters.

Accept that you cannot change what happened, but you can change how you feel about it.

Daily Self-Care Page

Morning

Approval

Evening

Forgiveness letter

Your ideas on how to take better care of your relationship/s

Insights

Affirmation

Daily Self-Care Page

Morning

Approval

Your ideas on how to take better care of your relationship/s

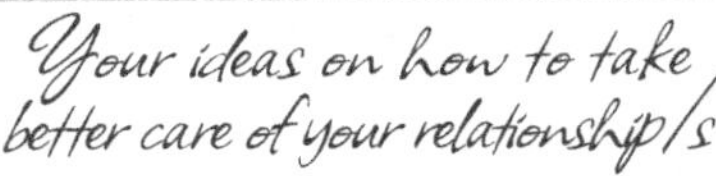

Evening

Forgiveness letter

Insights

Affirmation

DAY: TODAY'S MOOD:

Daily Self-Care Page

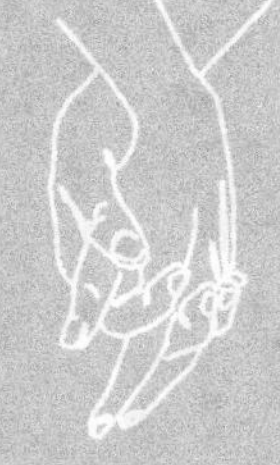

Morning

Approval

Your ideas on how to take better care of your relationship/s

Evening

Forgiveness letter

Insights

Affirmation

Daily Self-Care Page

Morning

Approval

Your ideas on how to take better care of your relationship/s

Evening

Forgiveness letter

Insights

Affirmation

Daily Self-Care Page

Morning

Approval

Evening

Forgiveness letter

Your ideas on how to take better care of your relationship/s

Insights

Affirmation

Daily Self-Care Page

Morning

Approval

Evening

Forgiveness letter

Your ideas on how to take better care of your relationship/s

Insights

Affirmation

Daily Self-Care Page

Morning

Approval

Evening

Forgiveness letter

Your ideas on how to take better care of your relationship/s

Insights

Affirmation

WEEK NINE

> *Sexuality is one of the ways
> that we become enlightened, actually,
> because it leads us to self-knowledge.*

Alice Walker

(Novelist)

Sensuality

Sensuality is the enjoyment, expression, savoring, or pursuit of physical, especially sexual, pleasure. Sensuality is linked with intimacy and involves feelings of emotional closeness and physical connectedness with your partner.

The biological and physical aspects of sexuality are concerned with the human reproductive functions, but it is more than that. Sexuality is not about who you have sex with or how often you have it. Sexuality is about romantic behaviors, desire, and passion. It is the feeling of being attracted to your partner: an expression of your body, emotions, and beliefs. It encompasses the dynamic you create in your intimate relationship.

You learned about intimacy from relationships around you, particularly within your family. Reflecting on the questions and bringing to light memories you carry in your mind and body completes your self-discovery journey.

Close your eyes, breathe, and connect with your pelvis. Answer the questions with openness:

1   How do you feel about your sexual energy?

2   What did you learn from your mother about
sexuality and intimacy?

3   What did you learn from your father about sexuality
and intimacy?

4   How was your first menstruation? What emotions
did you experience?

5   Is there something your pelvic area has to forgive?

6   What can you say about your health regarding
    your pelvic area?

7   Describe your first sexual experience:

8   Is your libido high or low?

9   What arouses you?

10 Are you disconnected from your body and from pleasure?

11 Do you like being touched?

____

____

____

____

12 How well do you know your body?

____

____

____

____

13 What kind of partners do you sexually attract?

____

____

____

____

14 How is your intimate life and how would you like
your sex life to be?

____

____

____

15 What can you do to become a better sensual partner?

____

____

____

____

Self-Care Practices

Be Sexy and Sensual

Own the power of your "Lady Garden"- a name for the female genitals. It is a beautiful term!

This area of your body has great power, once awakened.

Bring your attention to your "Lady Garden."

Feel the tingling that happens when you move your attention there.

Then smile at someone or give someone a compliment.

Notice what happens. Just the thought of this makes you smile, doesn't it?

Do this every day for seven days when you are with your partner, out for a coffee, or at work.

Peak Pleasure

Think back to three moments in your life when you experienced peak pleasure.

Take some time to relive those moments as if they were happening now.

Re-create the smells and sounds, the colors and the tastes, the sense of touch, and the emotional experiences you had. Your body makes no distinction between the actual event and what you imagine.

In re-creating these moments, you change the biochemistry of your body and release good hormones that make you feel great.

Remember that experiencing pleasure is crucial for vibrant health and sensuality.

Daily Self-Care Page

Morning

Be sexy and sensual

Evening

Peak pleasure

Your ideas on how to take better care of your sensuality

Insights

Affirmation

Daily Self-Care Page

Morning

Be sexy and sensual

Your ideas on how to take better care of your sensuality

Evening

Peak pleasure

Insights

Affirmation

# *Daily Self-Care Page*

DAY: TODAY'S MOOD:

Morning

Be sexy and sensual

Evening

Peak pleasure

Your ideas on how to take better care of your sensuality

Insights

Affirmation

Daily Self-Care Page

Morning

Be sexy and sensual

Evening

Peak pleasure

Your ideas on how to take better care of your sensuality

Insights

Affirmation

Daily Self-Care Page

Morning

Be sexy and sensual

Evening

Peak pleasure

*Your ideas on how to take
better care of your sensuality*

Insights

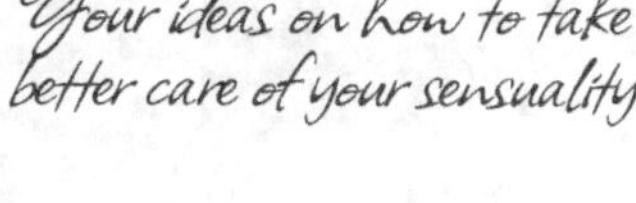

Affirmation

DAY: TODAY'S MOOD:

Daily Self-Care Page

Morning

Be sexy and sensual

Your ideas on how to take better care of your sensuality

Evening

Peak pleasure

Insights

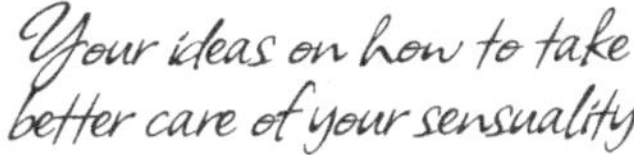

Affirmation

DAY: TODAY'S MOOD:

Daily Self-Care Page

Morning

Be sexy and sensual

Evening

Peak pleasure

Your ideas on how to take better care of your sensuality

Insights

Affirmation

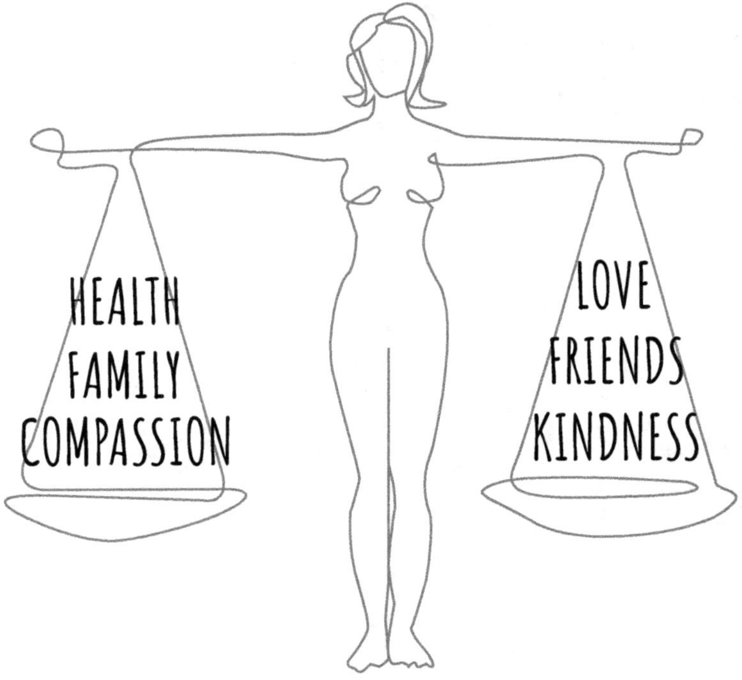

Values reflect what is important to the way you live and work.

(Anonymous)

Values

Values are your beliefs about what is morally right and wrong, as well as what is most important in life. Your values guide your life. All your decisions have values behind them.

You need to be aware of those values in order to define their degree of importance. You can find your values by analyzing your personal story, priorities, and how you spend your money and time.

If you don't know your values, you probably live your life according to other people's values or priorities.

Your values are also linked to how you feel. Suppose you feel unhappy, distressed, or dissatisfied about something. In that case, there's a good chance that your reality isn't living up to your expectations. Your dissatisfaction is often caused by a misalignment between your core values and what is happening in your life and work at the moment.

Go to your quiet place and let it flow:

1   What are your priorities in life?

2   What are you passionate about?

3   What would you do even if you didn't get paid?

4   When have you been most happy?

5   Which achievement or experience are you most proud of?

6 What has been your most significant success?

____
____
____
____

7 What has been your biggest failure?

____
____
____
____

8 Where does your money go?

____
____
____
____

9 How do you spend your free time?

____
____
____
____

10 What activities are you most interested in?

____
____
____
____

11   Are you satisfied with your life?

12   What are you hoping to achieve in life?

13   Think of a person you respect or look up to. What strengths or qualities do they have that you admire?

14   If you could have one wish fulfilled, what would that be?

15   What life changes would you need to make to accomplish this?

Exercise

Find Your Hidden Values

Describe your ideal day. Start with waking up and go hour by hour. Insert everything that you want to live your perfect day. At the end of this day, you are totally happy and satisfied. Your core values are hidden in your ideal day.

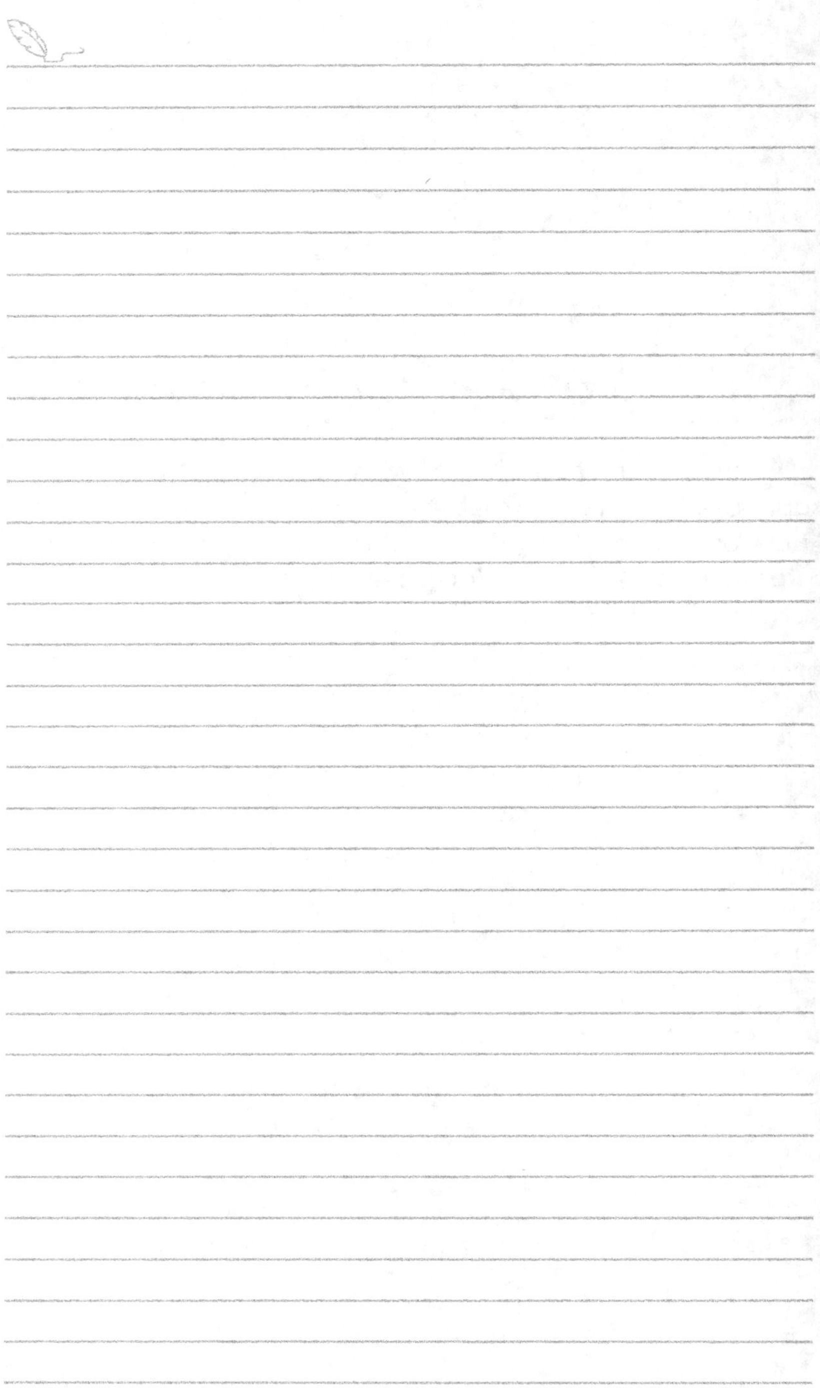

Write all the values you detected in your ideal day:

Congratulations on diving deeper into all the areas of your life we explored together!

All you wrote in this guided journal represents valuable information about yourself. Contemplate the content to see what pushed your buttons and why. When you bring these "programs" to the light, they no longer play in the background, shadowing your happiness. This means you are more conscious and free to decide for yourself.

Doing the self-care practices, you probably noticed a shift in how you feel. Continue practicing the ones you liked the most so you can be the happiest and best version of yourself.

Resources

Books

Goddesses Never Age: The Secret Prescription For Radiance, Vitality And Wellbeing by Dr. Christiane Northrup, Hay House, 2015

Why Kindness Is Good For You by David R. Hamilton PhD, Hay House, 2010

The Child In You: The Breakthrough Method For Bringing Out Your Authentic Self by Stefanie Stahl, Group Media Litera, 2019, 2020

Love Yourself And Let The Other Person Have It Your Way by Lawrence Crane and Lester Levenson, Lawrence Crane Enterprises, Inc. 2009

Change Me Prayers: The Hidden Power Of Spiritual Surrender by Tosha Silver, Atria Books, 2015

The Art Of Extreme Self-Care: Transform Your Life One Month At The Time by Cheryl Richardson, Hay House, 2009

Discover Sophrology For Your Wellbeing by Lorena Luchian, Amazon, 2018

References

https://www.goodreads.com/quotes/49864-and-you-when-will-you-begin-that-long-journey-into

https://www.goodreads.com/author/quotes/7049197.Doug_Cooper

https://www.goodreads.com/quotes/7685383-and-i-said-to-my-body-softly-i-want-to

https://www.goodreads.com/quotes/69994-all-the-things-that-truly-matter-beauty-love-creativity-joy

https://www.inspiringquotes.us/author/2408-lester-levenson/about-feelings

https://quotefancy.com/quote/1207829/William-Glasser-If-you-want-to-change-attitudes-start-with-a-change-in-behavior-In-other

https://positivepsychology.com/mindful-walking/

https://kaynutrition.com/why-cooking-is-self-care/

https://www.goodreads.com/quotes/376441-at-any-moment-you-have-a-choice-that-either-leads

https://quotefancy.com/quote/1680277/Jesse-Metcalfe-There-s-no-perfect-relationship-All-relationships-are-work-If-you-put-in

https://www.brainyquote.com/lists/topics/top-10-sexuality-quotes

https://slife.org/values-quotes/

https://therightquestions.co/what-are-your-personal-values/

About the Author:

Lorena Luchian (PsyD) is a licensed psychologist trained in Integrative Psychotherapy and Sophrology. She has been working in a medical clinic and private practice offering one-to-one and online sessions to her clients.

Lorena is the author of the book Discover Sophrology for Your Wellbeing and the author of articles and columns about mental disorders, self-help, sophrology, and women's health.

Due to her experience, she realized the importance of a holistic approach to health, which can be done at all levels of the personality: body, mind, emotions, behavior, and spirituality. Thanks to all her knowledge, her love for books, and her willingness to help other people discover who they are and find their balance, she is publishing books and beautiful journals for personal growth and the attainment of happiness.

Designed by
Mădălina Dumitrescu

Your feedback is very important to me. Please let me know how you liked the journal at:

luchianlorena.a@gmail.com

 lorena.luchian

 Lorena Luchian

9 783986 543044